Cal's Magical Clubs

by Ed Delgado   illustrated by Becky Fawson

Cielolindo Company

For Children everywhere-
Believing in yourself and never giving up
is Magical.

Text Copyright © 2021 by Ed Delgado
Illustrations Copyright © 2021 by Becky Fawson
Cover and book design Copyright © 2021 by Becky Fawson

Published by Cielolindo Company, Vienna, VA

All rights reserved. Including the right of reproduction in whole or in part in any form.

Printed in the USA

ISBN 978-1-09836-145-7

Cal was bored. That summer, his family moved to a new town and there were no other children in the neighborhood to play with.

Suddenly, Cal saw Pops coming to the front door!
Pops is his grandpa and very best pal.

He wrapped Cal in a big hug.

"I have a surprise for you," Pops said. "What is it?" Cal asked. Pops smiled and pulled out a small, white ball from his pocket. Cal was confused, but Pops kept smiling. "It's a golf ball! Come on son, we're going golfing!" Pops said. And off they went!

When they arrived at the golf course, Cal loved the rolling green hills, beautiful trees and the smell of fresh-cut grass.

Pops gave Cal some golf pointers and he started to get the hang of it. Cal had a blast smacking the balls all over the course.

"You are playing fantastic son! And, I have another surprise for you! Pops said.

He pulled out a new set of golf clubs just for Cal.
"Thank you so much, Pops!" Said Cal. "I'm going to play every day!"

After a great day on the golf course with Pops, Cal took his clubs home and cleaned each one of them. He brought his bag and clubs up to his room so he could watch over them.

The next day, Cal went back to the golf course to play by himself. He played for a while, but he was not doing too well. Without Pops there to help him, the game was much harder. Cal tried to be patient, but he was getting very discouraged.

He stomped his feet and said, "This game is no fun! Golf is too hard! I'll never learn to play like my Pops taught me. Forget it! I quit!"

Then he tossed his club on the grass.

Cal heard a voice. "Hey! What's the big idea, Cal?"

He could not believe his ears as he looked at his club. "D-D-Did you just t-t-talk?" He asked.

"Of course I just talked. We all do." Cal's club replied. "We'll introduce ourselves. I'm Decker the Driver. I have a long body and a big head. I'm the biggest and strongest club in the bag. You can use me when you tee up your ball and need to hit it far out on the fairway."

Next, three clubs popped out of the bag and said, "Hi Cal! We're the Iron brothers!"

The first club hopped forward and said, "I'm Freddy, the 5-iron."

"I'm Sammy, the 7-iron," said the middle club.

"Last but not least, I'm Nicky, the 9-iron. At your service," the last club said with a grin.

"Nice to meet you guys!" Cal said.

"We're not done yet, Cal. You still have some more friends to meet," said Decker the Driver.

"That's right," another club replied. "I'm Rudy, the Rescue Club and this is Sandy the Wedge. You can use us to get out of tough situations. Stuck in the tall grass? It's Rudy to the rescue!"

"If your ball is trapped in the sand, I'm your gal!" Sandy added.

Finally, the last club hopped out of the bag. It was light and small. "Hi there, I'm Patti the Putter and I'm here to finish the job!"

From one of the bag's pockets, a tee popped out and said, "I'm Taylor the Tee and I'm here to give you a lift when you need it!"

Cal looked around at all of his new friends and he could not wait to start playing again!

"Okay Cal, let's start our golf adventure and have some fun!" Said Decker the Driver.

Cal and his bag of clubs came up to the most challenging hole on the course. It was a long hole surrounded by water, trees and sand traps. Cal felt nervous. He was afraid that he would make mistakes in front of his new friends.

"I don't want to do this hole. It's too hard." Cal said.

"Don't worry buddy," said Decker the Driver. We can do this! If you believe in yourself, you can do anything that you put your mind to. Let's take it one step at a time and just have some fun."

"You're right, Decker. The hole may seem hard and I may not do well, but that's okay. I just want to do my very best! Plus, I have you guys to help me! So, let's play!" Cal said.

Cal put the ball on Taylor the Tee and lined up Decker the Driver.

"You can use me to hit the ball straight and over the water." Decker said.

He swung at the ball as hard as he could, but the ball didn't make it over the water.

Cal felt disappointed. "See, I'm no good at this. I should just quit."

"Now, now Cal," said Decker. "There's no need to feel down. It's okay to make mistakes on the golf course and in life. When you don't do well, you shouldn't give up. Just think positive and keep trying to do your best."

Cal felt better. "I'll give it another try." He said.

"Atta boy!" Decker said. "When you hit your last shot, you turned me in the wrong direction. This time, make sure that my face is straight and looking at the target. Relax, take a deep breath and swing!"

Cal relaxed but he teed the ball up too high and he hit Taylor the Tee instead of the ball.

"Whoa! That's quite a swing, Cal! Now all you have to do is hit the ball--not me." Taylor the Tee said with a smile.

At first, Cal felt embarrassed. But when he saw all of his friends smiling back at him, he smiled too.

"Okay guys, I think I'm going to get it this time." Cal said.

He faced Decker in the right direction, swung smoothly and hit a long shot over the water onto the middle of the fairway!

"Yay! Way to go Cal!" The clubs cheered!

Cal was excited and hurried over to his ball. Nicky, the 9-iron leaped out of the bag and said, "Hey, Cal! It's our time to shine! You can use me to hit the ball up and over the trees and sand trap!"

"Yes sir, Nicky! Cal said.

He set up Nicky, the 9-iron behind the ball and hit a beautiful shot.

His ball sailed over the trees, but landed right in the middle of the sand trap.

Cal lowered his head and said, "Oh, no . . . I'm in the sand. Whenever I get stuck in a trap, I can't hit a good shot to get out.

"It's alright, Cal," Nicky said. "The sand trap is tough, but you're tougher! You can hit the ball out! I believe in you!

"Okay Nicky. I'll do my best." Cal said, nervously.

Then, Sandy the Wedge came out of the bag and stood next to Cal. "I can help you here, buddy," she said. "The sand trap shouldn't be a problem for the two of us. Just relax and pretend you're on a nice sandy beach,"

Cal closed his eyes and swung Sandy the Wedge as hard as he could.

Sand went flying everywhere but the ball didn't budge.

Cal felt frustrated. He marched over to the ball, picked it up with his hand and tossed it out of the sand trap onto the short grass.

"There that's better," Cal said.

At first, the clubs looked at each other and were silent.

Then, Decker the Driver popped out of the bag and said, "Hold on, Cal, that's not being honest. You have to follow the rules of the game, even when it's not going your way. It's okay to feel frustrated, buddy. Just take a deep breath, calm down and try again."

Cal was still nervous, but he put the ball back in the sand and followed Decker's advice.

"Okay, just relax and swing easy under the ball." Cal thought to himself. He took a deep breath and swung Sandy under the ball and it landed right on the green!

When Cal and the clubs saw his shot, they all cheered!

"We knew you could do it, Cal!" Sandy the Wedge said. "Now it's time to finish the job!"

Patti the Putter jumped out of the bag and said, "My turn! It's time for the grand finale! Let's get the ball in the hole!"

Cal took Patti the Putter and lined up his putt.

He looked at the hole, then at his ball.

He relaxed and gently tapped the ball.

Cal and his clubs watched the ball
   roll...
       and roll...
           and roll...

IN THE HOLE!

They all jumped up and cheered!

"I can't believe it!" Cal said. "Thank you all for helping me and believing in me! You guys are the best friends anyone could ever ask for!"

"Don't mention it, Cal! We're a team!
We'll always be around to help you
on and off the golf course," Decker replied.

After a long day on the golf course, it was time for Cal to pack up his clubs and head home.

Decker the Driver said, "Hey buddy! We are all so proud of you! You hit some great shots today! And when you didn't, you learned to stay positive and keep trying.

"The most important part of any game is to do your best and have fun. You did exactly that, Cal. If you stay positive and always do your best, you can succeed at anything."

Cal smiled. "Even math?" He asked.

"Yes, buddy. Even math," Decker replied.

www.ingramcontent.com/pod-product-compliance
Lightning Source LLC
Chambersburg PA
CBHW061801290426
44109CB00030B/2913